This book
belongs
to

Cynthia Meidinger
21 September 1996

Illustrations by Hector Garrido
©The Bradford Exchange 1994

Stories and Introduction by Therese Lynn Johnson

Design by Maura Podrazik Gonsalves
Cover Design by Kathi D'Onofrio

Published by 🏛Roman, Jnc.
Roselle, Illinois

Printed and bound in the U.S.A.
ISBN: 0-937739-26-X

Visions
of Our Lady

Roman, Inc.

Ancient Prayer
to the Virgin

We turn to you for protection,
Holy Mother of God.
Listen to our prayers and
help us in our needs.
Save us from every danger,
Glorious and Blessed Virgin.

Introduction

She was known as Miriam to her small Jewish community nearly two millennia ago. She lived as a young woman of her culture, at one time, in one place. She is known to all ages thereafter as the Blessed Virgin, Our Lady, the Mother of God. She enters our world of limitations from her world that surpasses all time and place to communicate one universal message: peace. She knows all cultures, speaks all languages, lives in all ages. As a loving mother, she comes to warn her children of her Son's wrath and to beg them to repent and convert their hearts to love. But as a mother consoles her children, Our Lady speaks of the ultimate love her Son has for us.

We represent in this book a fraction of the chosen times in history Our Mother has appeared to her children. Although the year, the place, and the personalities change in each of her visits, Our Lady repeats one message: peace, penance, and conversion.

Contents

Our Lady of Lourdes

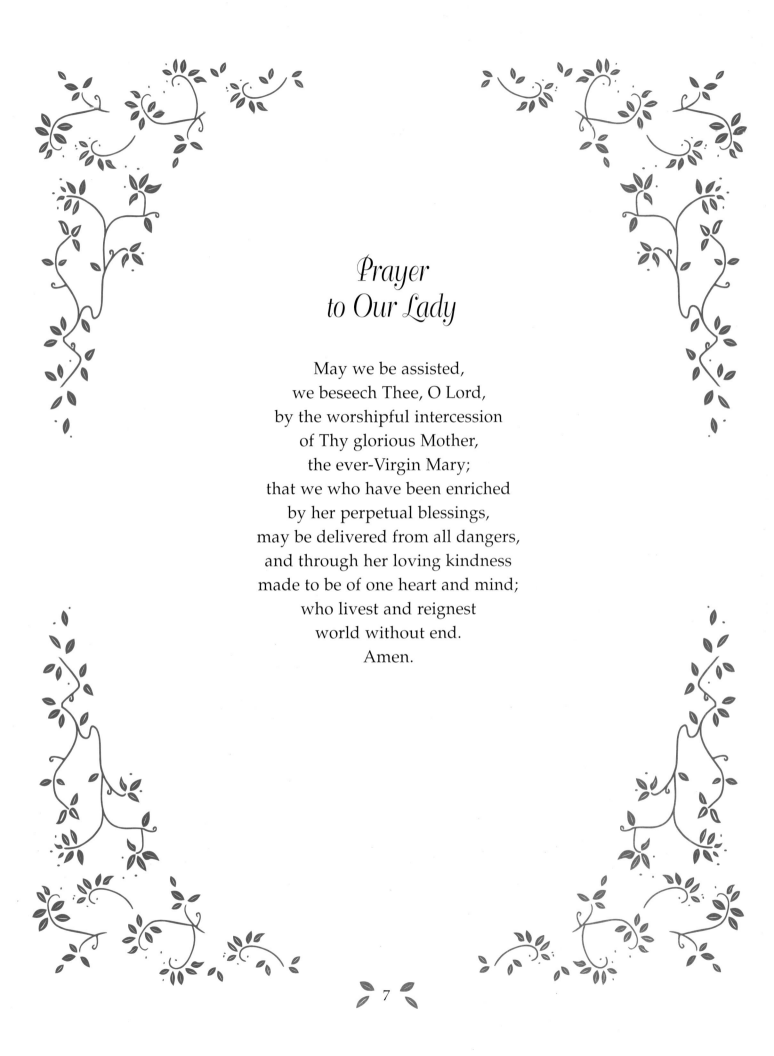

Prayer
to Our Lady

May we be assisted,
we beseech Thee, O Lord,
by the worshipful intercession
of Thy glorious Mother,
the ever-Virgin Mary;
that we who have been enriched
by her perpetual blessings,
may be delivered from all dangers,
and through her loving kindness
made to be of one heart and mind;
who livest and reignest
world without end.
Amen.

The Story of
Our Lady of Lourdes

Bernadette Soubirous had just reached Massabieille, a rocky area outside the village of Lourdes, France, when a terrible wind almost took her to the ground. She was with her sister, Toinette, and neighbor, Jeanne Abadie, gathering firewood for the family's next meal.

Before her eyes, in the niche of a rock grotto, stood a Beautiful Lady radiating like the sun's reflection through the clearest of crystals. She was dressed in an exquisite ivory robe, held to her waist by a deep sapphire sash. Pearl rosary beads draped from her delicate hands anchored in prayer. Framing the woman's devout face was a long ivory mantle trimmed in gold that flowed to her feet, on which rested two golden roses. Bernadette, mesmerized by the Lady's beauty and grace, could barely reach for her rosary. Not a word was spoken between the two on this day, February 11, 1858, the first of eighteen apparitions.

"Penance," the Lady said repeatedly to Bernadette in the apparitions that followed. "Pray to God for the conversion of sinners." As a gesture of penance, the Lady instructed Bernadette to drink and bathe from a certain place near the rock grotto. Seeing no water, Bernadette began to scrape up and drink the mud there. "I am doing this for sinners," she said to those in the surrounding crowd who accused her of being mad.

Although the young visionary did attract believers, many ridiculed her—among those, her mother. Bernadette half expected this response since the Lady had told her exactly one week after her first apparition, "I do not promise to make you happy in this world but in the next." Indeed, Bernadette did suffer humiliation and scorn from those closest to her.

The Lady issued Bernadette a second request: to have a chapel built on the site of her visits. The shy fourteen-year-old would have to approach the intimidating parish priest, the Abbé Peyramale, and convince him of the Lady's request; as with her mad act of drinking mud, Bernadette faced contempt. The abbé

demanded that she ask the Lady to identify herself, and if the young girl came back without an answer, he'd dismiss her visions as hallucinations.

Bernadette received her desired answer on the Feast of the Annunciation, March 25, 1858. "I am the Immaculate Conception," said the Beautiful Lady to the young girl. Ecstatic that she had an answer for the stubborn abbé, Bernadette started for the rectory. Although she, poor and uneducated, did not understand the words of the Lady, Bernadette repeated her message to the abbé, who anxiously awaited some made-up nonsense. Upon hearing the words *Immaculate Conception* he was convinced that the Mother of God had, indeed, been appearing to the young girl; he knew that the Church had just issued the doctrine regarding the Immaculate Conception, declaring that the Blessed Virgin was free of original sin from her conception.

The once-scorned Bernadette was, at last, vindicated in her lifetime. A small chapel dedicated to Our Lady of Lourdes was erected in 1866, two years after Bernadette joined the Sisters of Nevers. And the mudhole she had previously scraped, once the subject of much ridicule, now daily gushes forth 32,000 gallons of water that has healed and renewed thousands of believers. Lourdes has become the most popular healing and pilgrimage site in the world.

The apparitions at Lourdes were confirmed by the Church on January 18, 1862. Close to sixteen years later, in 1879, Bernadette Soubirous passed on, but her body, placed in the Sisters' chapel, has never decomposed. Bernadette was canonized December 8, 1933.

Our Lady of Medjugorje

Hail, Holy Queen

Hail, Holy Queen, Mother of Mercy:
hail, our life, our sweetness and our hope.
To thee do we cry,
poor banished children of Eve:
to thee do we sigh, mourning
and weeping in this vale of tears.
Turn then, most gracious Advocate,
thine eyes of mercy towards us
and, after this our exile,
shown unto us the blessed fruit
of thy womb, Jesus.
O clement, O loving,
O sweet Virgin Mary.

The Story of
Our Lady of Medjugorje

*I*t was a dry, hot afternoon when fifteen-year-old Ivanka and sixteen-year-old Mirjana decided to take a walk along the hills of their Yugoslavian village. As they neared the neighboring village of Medjugorje, Ivanka noticed atop Podbrdo Hill a celestial whitish-gray figure mysteriously turning.

"Could it be?" gasped Ivanka to Mirjana. "Could it be Our Lady?"

The following day, Ivanka, Mirjana, and four of their friends climbed the rough path toward Podbrdo Hill. They paused, in silence, at the bottom of the hill, afraid to move closer.

It was Ivanka who once again spotted the figure.

"Look, the Madonna!" Ivanka exclaimed more confidently than the previous day.

"She is calling to us," added Vicka, one of the friends.

All six children, pulled magnetically to what seemed to them the pinnacle of hope, ran up the steep incline. There they rested within a few feet of the most beautiful sight they had ever seen. The heavenly figure was clothed in snow-white clouds that matched her silk mantle, which extended beyond her length. Her crown of golden stars and silvery-azure dress made her almost indistinguishable from the sky against which she posed.

A sense of infinite peace came over them; all fears had vanished. The six, unable to take their eyes from her, knelt motionless in complete joy.

Smiling with enough love for all children in the world, she said to them on this second day, "Go in God's peace."

"I am the Blessed Virgin Mary," the Beautiful Madonna said to the six children the next day, June 26, 1981, her third visit. "Peace, peace, peace," she repeated. "Be reconciled." So attached is the message of peace and reconciliation to Mary's visits at Medjugorje that she became called the Queen of Peace. And prayer, fasting, and conversion are the means to peace.

Only four days after her first visit approximately 15,000 people gathered with the children on Podbrdo Hill, hoping to see for

themselves the Queen of Peace. Such a large crowd threatened Communist authorities, who first interrogated the children with psychiatric interviews, and then banned all gatherings at Podbrdo Hill. The apparitions eventually moved to a small room in the back of St. James Church.

The Queen of Peace still appears to some of the six visionaries, who anxiously await the rest of ten promised secrets: premonitions of world events and insight into what lies ahead. By December of 1982 Mirjana had already received all ten secrets. All six—Ivanka, Mirjana, Vicka, Milka, Jacov, and Ivan—are now married, and all but one live in or near their small village of Medjugorje.

Although Marian apparitions at Medjugorje are yet to be confirmed by the Church—or by the Diocese of Mostar—as "supernatural," their message has traveled to every nation; countless are the converts who have had their lives transformed in light of her presence and message. Over one million people have pilgrimaged to the site of today's apparitions.

Our Lady of Fatima

Novena
Prayer

Most holy Virgin,
who hast deigned to come to Fatima,
to reveal the treasures of graces
hidden in the recitation of the Rosary,
inspire our hearts
with a sincere love of this devotion,
that meditating on the Mysteries of
our Redemption recalled therein,
we may obtain the conversion of Russia.
And here name the other favors
you are praying for:
which we ask of you in this Novena,
for greater glory of God,
for your own honor,
and for the good of souls.
Amen.

The Story of
Our Lady of Fatima

Three shepherd children met one spring day in 1917 at the Cova da Iria—a meadow close to the village of Cabeço, Portugal—to tend their family flock, when mirror-like flashes of light struck close to them. Nine-year-old Lucia and her two cousins, Francisco and Jacinta, ran from what they assumed was lightning. As they ran, all six eyes spotted a brilliant sphere of light moving toward them, eventually landing atop a four-foot oak tree, or *carrasqueira*.

The three saw within the sphere a Beautiful Lady dressed in a pure white robe embroidered in a royal design and glimmering with golden highlights. She held a solemn expression, her eyes positioned intently on the pearl rosary that hung from her fragile wrists. The children, entranced by her utter grace and beauty, immediately fell to their knees and said prayers of adoration taught to them the summer before by a young man who had appeared to them three times and called himself the "Angel of Peace."

"Where do you come from?" asked young Lucia.

"I come from Heaven," the Lady responded with a love that would penetrate the most stubborn of hearts. She asked the children to return to the Cova on the thirteenth of each month.

Days passed and talk of the children's apparitions spread throughout their village and neighboring towns. Crowds soon accompanied the children to the Cova. The Lady spoke to the children about her Immaculate Heart and revealed to them the importance of the Rosary. "Say the Rosary to obtain peace for the world and the end of war," the Lady said. Repeatedly, Lucia later revealed, the Blessed Virgin asked the children to say special prayers for Russia. "I come to ask the consecration of Russia to my Immaculate Heart," Our Lady requested.

At her last appearance on October 13, more than 70,000 people witnessed a supernatural phenomenon: the sun plunged toward the earth and then, as if nothing had happened, returned to its proper place. This publicized event, the "Miracle of the Sun,"

convinced all of Portugal that the Immaculate Heart would indeed be its refuge.

Despite believing crowds, the three children faced interrogation from their families and civil authorities. A government administrator kidnapped the three, locked them away, and threatened them with death unless they revealed the secrets of the Lady. Afraid of nothing, even death, the children were set free; their unyielding faith rendered the authorities powerless. At home, Lucia endured the most difficult situation. Even after all the miracles witnessed by the children and people of their village, Lucia's mother remained profoundly skeptical.

It was Lucia who was chosen by the Virgin to spread worldwide devotion to the Madonna's Immaculate Heart. Francisco and Jacinta died at very young ages, as the Lady predicted would happen. In 1925 Lucia entered the convent of the Sisters of St. Dorothy, and a decade later wrote the first account of the apparitions.

The apparitions at Fatima were declared "worthy of belief" by the Church in 1930. Since then, many Holy Fathers have prayed special devotions to Mary's Immaculate Heart. Fulfilling the Lady's most adamant request, Pope Pius XII consecrated to her Immaculate Heart the people of Russia in 1952. In 1982, Pope John Paul II made his own pilgrimage to the basilica at Fatima in thanksgiving to the Immaculate Heart of Mary for his surviving an assassination attempt. Many people attribute the fall of Communism in Russia to all the prayers said in the name of Her Immaculate Heart, the great mission entrusted to Lucia at Fatima.

Our Lady of Guadalupe

Liturgical Prayer

God of power and mercy,
You blessed the Americas at Tepeyac
with the apparition of the
Virgin Mary of Guadalupe.
May her prayers help all men
and women to accept each other
as brothers and sisters.
Through Your justice present in our hearts,
may Your peace reign in the world.
We ask this through our Lord
Jesus Christ, Your Son,
Who lives and reigns
with You and the Holy Spirit,
one God, forever.
Amen.

The Story of
Our Lady of Guadalupe

"Juan, smallest and dearest of my little children, where are you going?" asked the Beautiful Girl to fifty-seven-year-old Juan Diego. It was Saturday, December 9, 1531, just before sunrise, when this Aztec Indian headed toward the small Mexican village of Tlaltelolco to attend Mass with the Franciscans.

Just as Juan skirted around Tepeyac Hill, he heard beautiful music, as if five separate choirs were performing in perfect harmony. He immediately stopped to listen, but the music abruptly ended—as if it depended on his movement. In the silence came a sweet voice urgently calling him: "Juan, Juan Diego, Juanito!"

Before him stood one of his own people—a Mexican girl, about fourteen years old—by far the most beautiful Aztec he had ever seen. Robed in exquisite garments, the young girl resembled an Aztec queen. She wore a scarlet gown adorned in a golden lace design; over her head and shoulders hung a deep jade mantle graced with saffron-gold stars. Gracefully poised, the beautiful Mexican balanced herself on a maroon crescent, lifted effortlessly by a cherub.

"Dear little son, I love you. I want you to know who I am. I am the ever-Virgin Mary, Mother of the true God who gives life," said the young girl. She requested a church be built on the hill for the Mexican natives, for whom she expressed a special love.

Despite his own crippling anxiety and initial scorn from the bishop's doormen, Juan managed to speak to the episcopal authority about the Lady's request but was dismissed without an answer. His second attempt was slightly more successful. "Let it be done," said the bishop, "if you can present me with a tangible sign from the Virgin, proof that she is the Mother of God and desires a church at the hill." Juan agreed immediately, certain that she would have a sign for him.

Juan's joyful anticipation and excitement lapsed immediately the next morning when he found his one remaining relative dying. He fetched a priest immediately for the Last Sacraments, but, ashamed

that he missed his appointment with the Virgin, avoided Tepeyac Hill.

"Forgive me," he explained to her when she intercepted him on the hidden path, "but my uncle is dying and desires the Last Sacraments." Touched by Juan's sincere compassion, the Virgin told him not to worry about his loved one and to attend to her mission.

She instructed him to gather in his overcoat, or *tilma*, the Castilian roses growing on the hilltop. Carefully, the Madonna arranged the roses, tied the corners of his coat, and warned him not to release the tight hold for anyone but the bishop.

The moment Juan had been anxiously waiting for came when he proudly untied the corners of his *tilma* before the bishop, who upon seeing it, fell to his knees in tears. Juan looked down to discover that the Virgin had entrusted him with an even more precious sign than the roses. There, on the front of his coat, was her image exactly as he had seen her. And when he returned home, Juan found his uncle restored to health; the Blessed Virgin had appeared to Juan's loved one, as well.

In only thirteen days a small chapel was completed for Our Lady of Guadalupe, and the *tilma* was carried forward in a festive procession; in the seven years that followed eight million natives were baptized. Today an average of 1,500 people daily kneel before the *tilma*, which has sustained its perfect image for almost 500 years, at the new Basilica of Our Lady of Guadalupe in Mexico City.

Our Lady of Grace

Memorare

Remember
O Most gracious Virgin Mary,
that never was it known that
anyone who fled to your protection,
implored your help,
or sought your intercession,
was left unaided.
Inspired with this confidence,
I fly to you,
O Virgin of virgins, my Mother.
To you I come,
before you I stand,
sinful and sorrowful.
O Mother of the Word Incarnate,
despise not my petitions,
but in your mercy
hear and answer me.
Amen.

The Story of
Our Lady of Grace

Twenty-four-year-old Catherine Labouré slept well every night at her new home, the motherhouse of the Daughters of Charity in Paris, France. Every night, that is, but July 18th, 1830, when she was awakened at half past eleven by a small boy about six years old.

"Come," said the boy, who was robed in pure white, "The Blessed Virgin awaits you!" This angelic figure radiated so brilliantly that the entire corridor through which he led the young novice glimmered with light. He directed her to the chapel, where, bowing before the Eucharist, was the Blessed Virgin. Catherine fell to her knees, placing her hands on the Madonna's knees.

"My child, God wishes to entrust a mission to you," said the Beautiful Madonna. But it wasn't until late November that Catherine discovered what exactly her mission would be.

That November evening at about 5:30, the chapel was completely still as the novices silently prayed. Catherine looked up immediately when she heard the same rustling of silk as she had heard on that memorable July night. There, on the right side of the altar, stood the same beautiful person she had met four months back. The Virgin wore a simple ivory gown, fit neatly to her waist and trimmed in gold at the neckline and cuffs; her auburn hair, peeking out from underneath a delicate white hood, framed her beautiful face. Her arms were wrapped in a soft blue mantle, and from her hands adorned with precious jewels—all sizes and colors—beamed forth luminous rays of light. The Lady balanced herself gracefully on a white sphere over which coiled a yellow-green serpent.

An oval frame gradually enclosed the Virgin, and around its border Catherine read the words: "O Mary conceived without sin, pray for us who have recourse to thee." Everything then reversed, and Catherine saw a large letter *M* surmounted by a bar and a cross, beneath which appeared the Immaculate Hearts of Mary and Jesus—one crowned with thorns, the other pierced with a sword.

"Have a medal struck after this model," an inner voice said to the novice. "All who wear it will receive great graces."

Learning about the mission was much easier than carrying it out, the young novice soon discovered after numerous attempts to have the medal made. She first approached Father Aladel, her confessor, who had great difficulty believing her story. He surmised that these made-up reports were, perhaps, a way for the shy, homely girl to feel important in her community.

The Blessed Virgin appeared to Catherine three more times, each time expressing her disappointment that no progress had yet been made on behalf of the medal. Catherine finally approached her confessor in tears, reporting the Lady's despondency. Taken by the girl's sheer distress, he approached the Archbishop of Paris, who, in a couple of months, had 1,500 medals made. Five years later, in Paris alone, more than two million medals had been struck, and it became known as the "Miraculous Medal."

Catherine did not admit in her lifetime that it was she who first saw Our Lady of Grace, the Lady of the Miraculous Medal, but her life of service and peaceful death evidenced her grace-filled encounters with the Mother of God. She was canonized July 27, 1947.

Our Lady of Mount Carmel

A Prayer to the Blessed Virgin

O Most beautiful Flower of Mt. Carmel,
Fruitful Vine, Splendour of Heaven,
Blessed Mother of the Son of God,
Immaculate Virgin,
assist me in this my necessity.
O Star of the Sea,
help me and show me
herein that you are my Mother.
O holy Mary, Mother of God,
Queen of Heaven and Earth,
I humbly beseech you
from the bottom of my heart,
to succour me in this necessity;
there are none that can
withstand your power.
Amen.

The Story of
Our Lady of Mount Carmel

Mount Carmel is the mystical pinnacle of the world, where the faithful have gathered since before Christ to hear the voice of Yahweh, the One God. Located on the border of Samaria and Galilee, twenty miles from Nazareth, this holy place holds a history extending far beyond any other Marian devotional site. This ascent was so famed for its beauty and fertility that it was called in Hebrew "the garden and vine of God."

Already in the fifth century, Christian hermits met at this heavenly garden to say prayers in honor of the Blessed Virgin. By the twelfth century, it had become a famed site of Marian devotion and the Order of Our Lady of Mount Carmel was founded.

Hermits affiliated with the Carmelite Order—who still met at the mountain to honor Our Blessed Lady—called themselves the Brothers of the Blessed Virgin Mary of Carmel, and, by 1220, had built a church on the fertile ascent in honor of her. Most of these brothers came to Europe shortly after, in the thirteenth century, and spread throughout the West devotion to Our Lady of Mount Carmel.

Tradition tells us that one Carmelite friar, St. Simon Stock, was in Aylesford, England, praying reverently to the Virgin Mary of Mount Carmel, when suddenly Our Lady herself appeared to him. The Beautiful Madonna held a brown scapular and with it promised, "This shall be a sign for you and for all Carmelites. Whoever dies in this shall not suffer eternal fire." Her words of consolation responded to Simon's desperate request that she help sustain the then oppressed order.

On this day, July 16, 1251, the prior general of the Carmelite Order saw Our Lady holding her Immaculate Son in her left arm. She wore a brown gown and white mantle, colors of the scapular that hung from her other arm. Her entire presence concentrated on the brown scapular, the privileged sacramental symbol attached to the Carmelites forever after. The scapular became understood by the Church as a miniature religious habit of the Carmelite Order, a constant reminder of the Blessed Virgin's presence.

It is the scapular devotion that is most significant in this apparition; devotion began with the apparition. "The scapular is the sign of salvation, a safeguard in dangers, a pledge of peace and of the Covenant," said the Blessed Virgin to Simon inside his humble cell. Just two centuries later all the faithful, not just Carmelites, were allowed to wear the scapular in devotion to the Mother of God. One of the oldest devotions to the Blessed Virgin, the wearing of the scapular became widespread in the Church for the next seven centuries, unto our day, and with it the promise of Our Lady of Mount Carmel. With this wide-spread devotion came the Feast of Our Lady of Mount Carmel, declared in 1726 by Pope Benedict XIII.

Ever since the Beautiful Madonna appeared to Simon, the first Carmelite Order and its affiliated orders have grown and flourished. They have been graced with the world's most profound mystics; in particular, John of the Cross, Teresa of Avila, and Therese of Lisieux. Carmelite spirituality has profoundly influenced all religious orders dedicated specifically to the Blessed Virgin and countless devoted laypersons.

The beautiful garden and vine of God remains today the spiritual center for all religious vocations following the example of Our Lady.

Our Lady of La Salette

La Salette
Invocation

Our Lady
of La Salette,
Reconciler of sinners,
pray without ceasing
for us who have
recourse to you.
Amen.

The Story of
Our Lady of La Salette

*I*t was 1846 and France was suffering tremendous social and political upheaval. Catholic churches had been abandoned and sacraments neglected. But away from the cities, in a high meadow along the French Alps, two cattle herders reverently knelt beside the Virgin Mary.

Eleven-year-old Maximin Giraud and fourteen-year-old Melanie Mathieu, employed separately by local farmers, met to graze livestock at a pasture in the small village of La Salette, France. This Saturday afternoon, as their cattle grazed in a nearby field, the two children shared bread and cheese alongside a peaceful ravine and then dozed off into a short slumber. They awoke after an hour and were hastily gathering their knapsacks when Melanie noticed a light near the ravine.

"Come quickly! See the light down there!" Melanie called out to Maximin. Both beheld a luminous sphere, radiating like the noon sun, curiously unfolding before their eyes. Gradually they made out a woman seated with her face in her hands, weeping. She gracefully arose and crossed her arms on her breast, her head somewhat inclined.

The children were drawn immediately to the woman's tears that adorned her face like perfectly cut diamonds glimmering in the sun's light. Her dynamic features were framed delicately in a white-satin headdress, on which rested a crown of roses: a bouquet of all shades of reds and pinks. A crucifix with pincers on one end and a hammer on the opposite end hung over her satin shawl, which was lined with more roses. The Madonna wore a long ivory dress embroidered in precious pearls and a yellow apron tied neatly to her waist. Wearing pearl slippers that peeked out from underneath her satin robe, she balanced herself atop a bouquet of roses.

"Come to me, my children," she tenderly addressed the two who stood afar, motionless. "Be not afraid. I am here to tell you something of the greatest importance."

As soon as they were within touching distance of her, she began to speak with the urgency of an ending world. "If my people will not obey, I shall be compelled to loose my Son's arm. It is so heavy, so pressing that I can no longer restrain it." She told the children that her Son was especially concerned that people were not keeping holy the seventh day, and that religion had lost its place in their country.

"You will make this known to all my people," she repeated to them.

This they did, unintentionally, through five years of exhaustive interrogation by the Bishop of La Salette, who had commissioned several committees to research the apparition. As the children repeated their story time and time again in perfect consistency people could not help but be convinced that the Blessed Virgin had appeared to the two. Churches began to fill throughout neighboring villages and the Catholic faith resumed some of its deserved respect. On the first anniversary of the apparition nearly 60,000 people prayed together on the mountain of the Marian site.

A little more than five years after Mary's first and only appearance at La Salette, the apparition was officially approved by the Church, and nearly thirty years after that the basilica erected in the name of Our Lady of La Salette was completed and consecrated. Maximin and Melanie were not canonized by the Church, but throughout their lives they continued to serve as witnesses to Our Lady and to transmit her message.

Virgin of the Poor

Novena Prayer

O Most blessed Mother,
heart of love, heart of mercy,
ever listening, caring, consoling,
hear our prayer.
As your children
we implore your intercession
with Jesus, your Son.
Amen.

The Story of
Virgin of the Poor

I t was a bitter January night in a small Belgian hamlet, where eleven-year-old Mariette waited anxiously for her younger brother Julien to return from an errand. This Sunday night, January 15, 1933, just outside the village of Banneux, young Mariette peered out of the large front window of her house hoping to locate at least a hint of movement, when her eyes were drawn to a glistening light near her mother's small vegetable garden. Within the light she made out a Beautiful Lady graciously smiling.

"Ah," the young girl gasped with reverent awe and fascinated wonder. "Mama, there's a woman in the garden!"

Determined to get a better view, Mariette reached for her coat and hat on her way out the door when her mother intercepted and locked the door. She, too, looked outside the window but made out no figure. And when little Julien finally returned home, he joined his mother in mocking the vision of his sister.

However, young Mariette's behavior was so atypical during the week she saw the apparition that her entire family was convinced something real had occurred on that snowy Sunday evening. The formerly indifferent girl prayed at her parish church before school each morning and recited perfectly her catechism at the class she used to skip.

After the next apparition, only four days after the first, Mariette was able to describe the Madonna to her pastor with better detail. On this Wednesday evening the Lady appeared only five feet away from the child, who knelt joyfully praying the Rosary. Between two frosted pines the Madonna stood atop a silver cloud ascended only a foot from the ground. She wore a deep blue sash around the waist of her pearl-white gown, which flowed to her bare feet on which rested one golden rose. A thin translucent veil, almost indistinguishable from the oval light surrounding her, framed her delicate features. The Lady moved her lips, as if she was joining Mariette in the Rosary, but didn't touch the crystalline beads that hung from her right arm.

This night Mariette's father, Julien, watched the child welcome the Virgin. As he returned from gathering two other witnesses, Mariette was making her way down the road—as if she was being pulled—toward a small stream close to the house. "She is calling me," she simply explained to her father. Instructing the young girl to place her hands in the water, the Virgin said to her, "This stream is reserved for me."

"I am the Virgin of the Poor," the Beautiful Madonna identified herself to young Mariette the next night, the third of eight visits. Under that title she requested a small chapel be built and dedicated at Banneux.

For the next three weeks Mariette prayed the Rosary each night in the cold, waiting anxiously for the Beautiful Lady, who did not appear again until February 11th. At school Mariette suffered much ridicule and scorn. Schoolmates and village neighbors had difficulty believing the Mother of God would appear in a vegetable garden, literally next to the cabbage, to a girl who did not even know her catechism.

But as skeptics multiplied so did believers, and devotion to the Virgin of the Poor spread rapidly. In 1949, the Bishop of Liege announced the formal approval of the apparition after recommendation from a committee commissioned to research the visions. Since then, at least 150 small chapels have been dedicated to the Virgin of the Poor, duplicates of the humble chapel erected in August of 1933, just eight months after Mariette's first apparition.

The young visionary did not feel called to religious life, but her devotion to the Virgin of the Poor has been as profound as the first night she encountered her.

Virgin with the Golden Heart

Immaculate Heart of Mary

O Most pure Heart of Mary,
full of goodness,
show your love toward us.
Let the flame of your heart, O Mary,
descend on all people.
We love you immensely.
Impress on our hearts true love
so that we long for you.
Amen.

The Story of
Virgin with the Golden Heart

*I*t was a damp, clammy November evening in 1932, when four Belgian children walked to the convent of the Sisters of Christian Doctrine. Eleven-year-old Albert and his older sister, Fernande, first set out for the Degeimbre household to pick up young Gilberte and Andree Degeimbre. It had become routine for the four children to pick up Gilberte Voisin, the younger sister of Albert and Fernande, from the Sister's academy where she attended class. Nothing was out of the ordinary this Tuesday evening, November 29, in the small Belgian village of Beauraing until the four reached the door of the convent.

After Albert rang the bell, he turned toward the street and saw a luminous figure walking above the bridge by the Lourdes grotto inside the convent yard. "The Virgin dressed in white is walking above the bridge!" he exclaimed to the others, who, because the boy joked often, did not believe a word. The three anticipated an outbreak of laughter. Surprised by his self-constraint and seriousness, they turned around for themselves and saw the same vision.

The four pounded frantically at the door until Sister Valeria arrived. Gilberte Voisin looked immediately to the place where four hands pointed and saw the Lady. But Sister Valeria, seeing nothing, called them foolish, as did the mother of Gilberte and Andree upon hearing their report. "Don't tell any of this foolishness to your parents," she warned the three Voisin children. Yet, not even inside the door, the three blurted out what they had just seen to their parents, who sent them straight to bed after a scolding.

When the children returned from their errand the next evening with the same story, Mrs. Degeimbre, convinced that some trickster was behind the illusions, decided to investigate the mystery and, with other adults, began to escort the children.

"She is here," gasped one of the children spotting the figure on the walk between the convent gate and the front door. The young

visionaries saw more clearly her overwhelming beauty. She wore a simple ivory gown that flowed gracefully to her feet, which were hidden in a snow-white cloud. A glimmering light framed perfectly her silk mantle that draped over her head like a wedding veil. Her arms were extended in a permanent embrace to the children. The Lady appeared four times this night—the last time near a rose hawthorn tree in the convent garden, where she appeared from then on.

The Sisters, nervous that the diocese would soon learn of the stories, severely warned the students about any talk of the visions. And to further discourage any activity on the premises, they locked the gates of the academy and released dogs in the convent yard. But despite the nuns' efforts, more and more people joined the children on the convent grounds. On the evening of the Feast of the Immaculate Conception, just nine days after the Virgin's first appearance, nearly fifteen thousand people gathered behind the gates of the academy.

The Lady who had by now defined herself as the Immaculate Virgin continued to visit the children, but less frequently. On the last day of the year she revealed her golden heart to all five children. Nearly 35,000 people gathered to witness the Madonna's last appearance on January 3, 1933, when she told each of the children secret messages and, in a gesture of farewell, displayed her golden heart.

As was first anticipated by the Sisters, the Bishop of Namur, alerted by the reports, commissioned a committee to research the apparitions. After fourteen years and seventy-two sessions, the apparitions were approved on July 2, 1949, two years after the erection of a small chapel at the site.

All five children married and started their own families, drifting occasionally back to the hawthorn tree in the convent garden, where thousands of pilgrims pray each year to Our Lady of the Golden Heart.

Our Lady of Hope

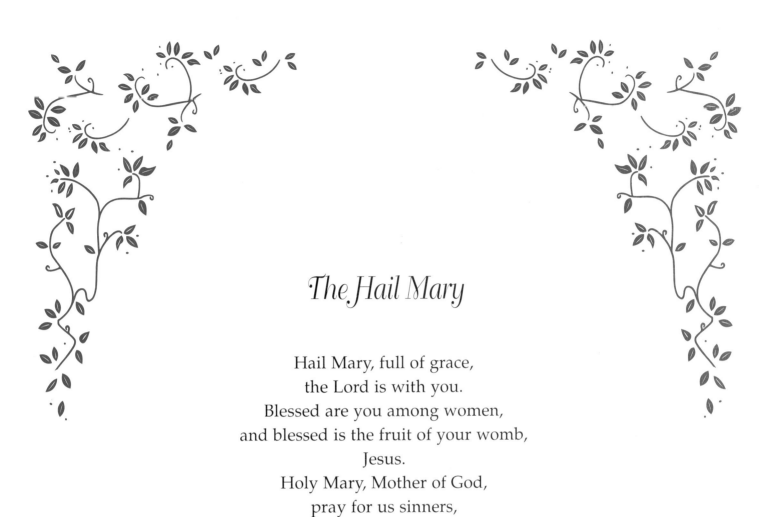

The Hail Mary

Hail Mary, full of grace,
the Lord is with you.
Blessed are you among women,
and blessed is the fruit of your womb,
Jesus.
Holy Mary, Mother of God,
pray for us sinners,
now and at the hour of our death.
Amen.

The Story of
Our Lady of Hope

Twelve-year-old Eugene Barbadette rose early one January morning in 1871 to wake his younger brother, Joseph. The two French boys prayed the Rosary each morning for their older brother, Auguste, who had been called to battle. All five hundred or so villagers of Pontmain—a small French hamlet about two hundred miles west of Paris—talked about nothing other than the ill-fated war with Prussia that had begun only six months prior.

"God will have pity on us; his mercy will surely come to us through Mary," the Abbé Guerin said to his congregation the morning of January 17th. The pastor lived an uncommon devotion to Our Lady and expressed hope to villagers in the midst of great despair. Not even one day passed before his words at Mass actualized in a vision of Our Lady.

That evening Eugene and Joseph were busy helping their father feed the animals in the barn when a neighbor interrupted with wonderful news: Auguste was safe. Eugene walked toward the door and gazed with gratitude into the winter's sky. His eyes were immediately drawn to one dark vacuum void of stars. Suddenly, in place of constellations, appeared a Beautiful Woman wearing golden stars on her deep blue garment. She seemed a part of the sky, yet distinguished from it by her striking beauty.

Eugene's mouth dropped open in awe. His curious brother soon stood with him entranced by the vision. The two described her to their father and neighbor in perfect consistency. Over her ocean-blue gown adorned with golden stars draped a sable-lavender mantle. The cloak flowed from her head, crowned with shimmering gold and precious jewels, to her matching slippers. Her uncommon poise and exquisite garments evidenced her unprecedented nobility. She balanced herself gracefully on a small cloud suspended just above the house opposite the Barbadette's.

The two witnesses and two more who had joined them looked over the boys' shoulders but saw nothing. Sister Vitaline, who later

came with the boys' mother, went to seek two other children, Françoise Richer and Jeanne-Marie Lebosse, guessing that the vision might only be visible to children. The children saw the woman immediately and, without prior information, described her exactly as had the Barbadette boys.

Only twenty minutes later, a crowd gathered near the Barbadette barn, and, as the Sister had surmised, only children saw the Lady. Even the Abbé Guerin, extremely dedicated to Our Lady, could not see her. As the abbé recited the *Magnificat*, the children read from a large white banner that had begun to unroll just below her feet: "But pray, my children, God will hear you in a little while." This single apparition at Pontmain lasted about three hours.

Our Lady's message of consolation lifted all hearts weighted by the fear of losing their loved ones to battle. And no longer did the villagers fear Prussia's impending invasion into their Diocese of Laval. As the abbé had said just that morning, God had shone his mercy through Mary and had heard the prayers of the community. Within eleven days the Prussians had mysteriously withdrawn all troops from France and the war was over. Although France did suffer severe repercussions of the war, the faithful village of Pontmain was saved and their loved ones returned home safe.

Only one year after the apparition, the Bishop of Laval approved the apparition and made plans to erect a shrine on the very spot where Our Lady appeared. A large church, named Our Lady of Hope, was built in 1872 and later consecrated and designated as a basilica.

Three of the four visionaries entered religious life; the other became a schoolroom assistant. And the barn of the Barbadettes, where all four encountered Our Lady, was maintained and converted into a simple chapel.

Our Lady of Silence

Regina Caeli

Queen of heaven, rejoice,
Alleluia.
The Son you merited to bear,
Alleluia,
has risen as he said,
Alleluia.
Pray to God for us,
Alleluia.

Rejoice and be glad,
O Virgin Mary,
Alleluia.
For the Lord has been truly risen,
Alleluia.

The Story of
Our Lady of Silence

*I*t was raining furiously the night of August 21, 1879, in the village of Knock, Ireland. Mary Byrne was walking home a visitor, Mary McLoughlin, the housekeeper of the parish priest. The two women had just reached the wall surrounding the church grounds when Mary Byrne noticed a curious light near the south end of the church.

"Look at the beautiful statues!" she exclaimed to her companion, upon seeing three figures standing out from the gable, about two feet off the ground. As both walked toward them they were practically blinded by the light that was growing brighter with each step. Both at first assumed their pastor, Archdeacon Cavanaugh, had purchased new statues. But upon moving closer they saw the figures move and were eventually able to identify them. Although the grass and everything surrounding the gable was drenched, the figures and the entire gable remained miraculously dry and untouched by the south winds.

"It's the Blessed Virgin!" exclaimed Mary Byrne to her companion. The two stood motionless before the Madonna, the largest figure of the three. To her left stood what appeared to be Saint John the Evangelist, and to her right Saint Joseph.

Our Lady, robed in dazzling white, stood erect with her arms extended upward and her eyes gazing toward her home in the heavens. Over her simple dress she wore a pearl-ivory cloak, which fell gracefully in full folds to her bare ankles. More noble than any queen, she was crowned in shimmering gold; a coronet of ornate crosses graced her head. The three figures shone like glistening silver.

Within an hour the entire Byrne family and about a dozen other people gathered around the south gable, watching, praying, and quietly discussing the scene. Unlike other Marian apparitions, all witnesses—children and adults alike—could see the figures and experienced the overwhelming love they exuded. After two hours

the silent apparition ended; the figures mysteriously disappeared, as they had come.

A commission was created within several months by the Archbishop of Tuam—the diocese to which Knock belongs—to interview about fifteen of the approximate twenty witnesses. The Archbishop, after reviewing evidence supporting the apparition, made no statement for or against Knock. As his health failed, he remained extremely skeptical, especially since no words were spoken or messages given. But to Irish believers, the vision was full of meaning. Saint John's dress reiterated the sacred role of the priest and the authority of the official church, which were both tested at that time. And Saint Joseph's role as patron of the Church and protector of Jesus and Mary comforted all Irish Catholic families.

Many of the original witnesses died before a second commission, more than fifty years after the first, reopened the investigation. Still no official statement of approval was made by the subsequent Archbishop of Tuam, but he began to take part in the pilgrimage devotions and explained that since no statement was made by his predecessor, Catholics could follow their own convictions regarding the apparition. The visit of Pope John Paul II in 1979 and other privileges extended to the shrine at Knock strengthened the Church's sanction.

The once quiet village of Knock was—within a year of the apparition—visited by pilgrims from all over Ireland and the United Kingdoms. So big were the crowds that in 1976 a larger church, the Church of Our Lady Queen of Ireland, was dedicated to Knock. About one million pilgrims annually visit Knock today.

Our Lady of Snows

My Queen, My Mother

My Queen, my Mother,
I give myself entirely to thee,
and to show my devotion to thee,
I consecrate to you this day
my eyes, my ears,
my mouth, my heart,
my whole body
without reserve.
Amen.

The Story of
Our Lady of Snows

The legend of Our Lady of Snows dates back to the fourth century. During the night of August 4th, in the year 352, the Blessed Mother appeared to a wealthy, elderly couple in Rome who had made the Virgin Mary their heiress! The noble pair desperately wanted a son or daughter, an heir to whom they could leave their assets, but after childbearing years were left without any. They grew old, and, knowing their last days were approaching, prayed to the Blessed Virgin to show them how she wanted to use her inheritance.

In their dreams this August night, the Madonna appeared and requested a basilica be built on the Esquiline Hill, one of Rome's seven hills, on the exact spot that she would designate with snow. She appeared the same night to Pope Liberius and requested the same.

The next morning, August 5th, the city arose to a summer snowfall. A blanket of snow miraculously carpeted Esquiline Hill. The wealthy couple met Pope Liberius at the mystical hill, who upon seeing the Virgin's awesome sign, at once dug the basilica's foundation. After the exact site for the basilica had been staked off, the snow disappeared immediately. Excitedly, the couple watched their generous gift materialize into the first and greatest church in Rome dedicated to Our Lady. To this day it is the principal Roman church erected in Mary's honor.

The basilica, named Saint Mary Major on account of its size and splendor, was restored and enlarged by Pope Sixtus III a century after its founding. The exquisite church celebrates Mary's divine motherhood, symbolized by a triumphal arch erected in the basilica immediately after the Council of Ephesus, which confirmed Mary's divine motherhood. The enamel arch, adorned with Rome's finest mosaics, extends almost seventy feet and expresses in symbolic art the triumphal history of the Mother of God; depicting scenes in Mary's life, the arch and the walls of the nave tell her biography. Through the centuries various popes and

episcopal leaders have taken great joy in adorning the church, a way of honoring Mary's motherhood.

So majestic is the basilica that it houses in its famous Pauline Chapel the most honored icon of Our Lady, a painting attributed to Saint Luke. Different popes have spent entire nights in front of the image in veneration to the Mother of God, and three have crowned the icon, a gesture that celebrates Mary's divine motherhood. The holy painting, now referred to as Our Lady, Protectress of Rome, has been used as a shield in Rome's history, a source of strength and protection for Roman citizens through the centuries. Copies of the icon have been believed to be miraculous.

In the seventeenth century Pope Pius V declared the Feast of Our Lady of Snows, which is celebrated August 5th of each year, the anniversary of the basilica's founding. During the feast day Mass at the basilica, a shower of white rose petals falls from the church ceiling in remembrance of the miraculous snowfall that, tradition holds, designated the exact site and size of the church.